CONTENTS

KT-564-946

Witnesses to War   4

Stories from the First World War   6

Museum History   10

Stories from the Second World War   12

Peace and Security   18

Secret War   22

Art   24

Extraordinary Heroes: The Lord Ashcroft Gallery   26

The Conservation Lab   28

For Grown-Ups Talking to Children About War   30

Other IWM branches   31

Quiz and Wordsearch   32

WITNESSES TO WAR

These are some of the biggest and most impressive objects in the building. Look up, down and all around to see these amazing objects from all angles.

You'll be glad to hear that the objects hanging from the ceiling are supported by very strong cables. They have to be checked regularly, and are strong enough to carry at least twice the weight of the objects they hold. So no need to worry about aeroplanes dropping on your head!

FIND IT!

Can you see the holes in this gun? They were caused by German shells hitting the gun in a fierce battle in September 1914

The V2 rocket is the tallest object in the museum. How many people of your height would need to stand on each other's heads to reach from the bottom to the top? (*Clue: the V2 is 14.02m tall.*)

Invented by Nazi scientists in Germany, the V2 rocket could hurtle from northern Europe to Britain in just a few minutes. A V2 destroyed a building opposite IWM London in January 1945.

This Book Belongs To

....

FIVE HIGHLIGHTS!

5 LORD ASHCROFT GALLERY

4 HOLOCAUST EXHIBITION

3 ART

2 PEACE AND SECURITY / SECRET WAR

1 SECOND WORLD WAR STORIES

0 FIRST WORLD WAR STORIES

1

WELCOME

Welcome to IWM London!
IWM (Imperial War Museums) was set up nearly 100 years ago to remember the work and struggles of the people of Britain and its Empire in the First World War. Today we tell the story of how war has changed our world and how people's lives have been affected by war.

This guidebook will help you get the most out of your visit, and to think about it after you've left.

Look out for:

- The 'Find It' sign, which shows you special things to look for in the galleries

  FIND IT!

- Sticker activities, using the sticker sheet at the back of the book

  STICKER IT!

- 'Start a Conversation': questions to get you talking with your family about what you've seen (there are helpful hints for grown-ups on page 30)

  Start a Conversation

- 'Fun Facts' to boggle your mind and impress your friends

  Fun Fact

- Activities to do either as you go around the museum, or later on at home

  DRAW IT!

Fun Fact

We have around 10 MILLION objects in our collections!

This includes small items like letters, diaries and photos, as well as the big things like tanks and aeroplanes.

Unlike most aircraft, the Harrier Jet can take off and land vertically (straight up in the air). This Harrier flew in Afghanistan, helping British soldiers to fight the Taliban in 2004 and 2006.

HOW TO CLEAN AN AEROPLANE

All the objects on display get dusty, and they have to be cleaned to protect them. But how do you dust an aeroplane that's hanging out of reach?

The answer is a 'spacevac' — not a futuristic hoover-robot, but a vacuum cleaner with extra-long tubes. The IWM team use the spacevac standing on the floor to clean the V2 rocket, and from the side galleries on Level 3 to get to each end of the Harrier Jet.

Start a Conversation

Do you think it would be exciting to be a war reporter?

In 2006 two journalists were driving this armoured Land Rover in Gaza, where the Israelis were fighting the Palestinians. When the car was fired on by an Israeli helicopter, they were badly injured. If you stand on the stairs above, you can still see the damage to the car. Why do you think 'TV PRESS' is written in big letters all over the Land Rover? Why did the journalists want everyone to know who they were?

Full Fact

To help them decide which objects should go into the Witnesses to War space, the IWM team made 'fuzzy felt' versions of all the possible objects. By moving the fuzzy felt versions around, they could work out what would fit and where!

STORIES FROM THE
FIRST WORLD WAR

This famous face belongs to Lord Kitchener, the war minister. It was his job to get people to sign up for the army. Check your height in the gallery to see if you pass his test!

1914'S MUST-HAVE PRESENT

EVERY CHILD SHOULD HAVE ONE!

PROPELLERS REALLY TURN!

Toy battleships were all the rage in 1914 in Germany. Parents bought them to show they were proud of their country and its navy, which they hoped would soon be as powerful as Britain's.

Do you have any war toys? Do you think this would be fun to play with?

ALFIE'S WAR AMBITION

AUGUST 1914: 9-YEAR-OLD ALFIE KNIGHT IS WRITING TO A VERY IMPORTANT PERSON

DEAR LORD KITCHENER. I AM AN IRISH BOY 9 YEARS OF AGE AND I WANT TO GO TO THE FRONT. I CAN RIDE JOLLY QUICK ON MY BICYCLE AND WOULD GO AS A DISPATCH RIDER.

I AM VERY STRONG AND OFTEN WIN A FIGHT WITH LADS TWICE AS BIG AS MYSELF. I WANT A UNIFORM AND A REVOLVER...

LORD KITCHENER REPLIED:

I AM AFRAID YOU ARE NOT QUITE OLD ENOUGH TO GO TO THE FRONT!

Did anyone in your family fight in the First World War?

Do you know what happened to them?

Often, people who fought in the war didn't talk much about it. Perhaps the experience was too horrible, or they thought no-one would understand. Some people only found out their family members' war stories many years later.

This collar was worn by a messenger dog called Wolf! The collar carried messages on rolled-up paper. Dogs could run quickly and were harder for the enemy to see, so they were used to carry messages in the trenches – just like the dog in the photo. Around 20,000 dogs served with the British Army.

Fun Fact

All sorts of animals served in the First World War, from horses, dogs and pigeons to camels in the desert. There was even a plan to train sealions to follow enemy submarines – but the sealions weren't that interested.

Oppy Wood, 1917. Evening, by John Nash, 1918

A German messenger dog jumping over a trench, France, 1917

Camouflage trees were used to spy on the enemy from 'no man's land' in between the two lines of trenches. A pretend tree was made from metal, cloth and paint to look like one in no man's land. At night, soldiers would sneak out, cut down a real tree and put the fake one in its place.

Does this camouflage tree look like trees near where you live? Why do you think it doesn't have any leaves?

FIRST WORLD WAR

LEVEL

0

7

STORIES FROM THE
FIRST WORLD WAR

You've heard of a piggy bank? Well, this is a tank bank. The British Army started using tanks in 1916, and were very proud of them. The government wanted everyone at home to save and give money to help Britain win the war. They needed lots of cash to buy food, clothes, equipment and weapons (including tanks!) for the army.

STICKER IT!

'Practically the whole time you had to sleep with your boots on in case things went wrong anywhere.'
Private Reginald Haine

A white feather in the First World War meant someone was a coward. This feather was sent in the post to a man who disagreed with the war. Sometimes women handed white feathers to men in the street who weren't in uniform, to embarrass them by saying they were too scared to fight.

Why do you think some men wouldn't want to fight?

Noble Sir. If you are too proud or FRIGHTENED. Co FIGH wear this.

Soldiers could be in the trenches for a long time – cold and damp in the winter, hot and dusty in the summer. They loved to get parcels from home. At Christmas 1914, soldiers in the British Army were given tins by the King's teenage daughter, Princess Mary. The tins held presents such as cigarettes, sweets and writing sets.

Add your own Princess Mary tin here using the sticker from the back of this book.

Imagine you are fighting in the trenches. What would you like to have in a parcel sent from home?

FIND IT!

Get a feel for life as a First World War soldier by trying on the uniforms in the gallery.

'...every man in the front line had fleas after about two or three weeks.'
Private Clifford Lane

By 1917 the British Navy had a big problem. German submarines were destroying their ships. Artist Norman Wilkinson had a bright idea to help British ships stay safe at sea – he made them confusing to look at. His crazy 'dazzle' patterns made it hard for the enemy to see which way the ship was going and even how big it was.

Colour in the ships to dazzle the enemy. Here's an example:

MUSEUM HISTORY

The Imperial War Museum was set up to remember how the people of Britain and its Empire fought and suffered in the First World War. Over the years the museum has collected all sorts of things, including weapons, uniforms, letters, photographs, vehicles and even stuffed animals!

This advert appeared in ration books in 1918, asking people to send in donations.

In the Second World War, the armed forces were so short of guns and equipment that in 1940 people from the British Army and Navy took away some of the old guns from the galleries to use again!

Full Fact

IMPERIAL WAR MUSEUM

The Imperial War Museum desires to receive for permanent preservation photographs and biographical material, printed or in manuscript, of all officers and men who have lost their lives or won distinctions during the War; also original letters, sketches, poems and other interesting documents sent from any of the war areas, and all kinds of mementoes, even of trifling character, which may be of interest in connection with the War.

They should be sent to:

THE SECRETARY,
Imperial War Museum,
Great George Street,
Westminster, S.W.1.

MOVING HOUSE
In 1920 the museum opened in the grand Crystal Palace in south London, but a few years later it had to move to a smaller place in South Kensington. When the museum moved to its current home in 1936, it took the curators and a team of soldiers six weeks to move all the objects in!

Even in a war museum, bombs are not always a good thing. The museum received an unwanted object in the Second World War, when a German aeroplane dropped a bomb straight into the galleries. Luckily no-one was badly hurt, but a First World War aeroplane and many model ships were destroyed.

When the museum was set up, Britain was still fighting the First World War. It was the perfect time to gather objects from the war, but collecting them would mean going to dangerous places! Major Henry Beckles Willson from Canada was chosen as the man for the job. He set off for France in 1917. He wanted to show what the war was like for ordinary soldiers.

Beckles Willson chose the objects he wanted for the museum and sent them back to London. Objects were also collected from other fronts like Palestine and Salonika in Greece.

Nearly 100 years after Beckles Willson went to France, IWM were collecting in a war zone again. Project manager Louise Skidmore, photographer Richard Ash and video cameraman Damon Cleary made three trips to Afghanistan in 2012–14. It wasn't easy. They drove through a sandstorm on one visit, and a snowstorm on another! They worked hard, but they also had fun – they even won a pub quiz at an army base camp!

Louise, Damon and Richard with their army liaison officer.

ACTIVITY

Do you think these items were collected by Beckles Willson or Louise Skidmore? Tick who you think it was.

▲This steel helmet belonged to a soldier named William Short, who earned a Victoria Cross for fighting in France.

▲ The embroidery on this dress shows that local crafts were being used to help people earn money in Afghanistan.

◄ This lamp was made by prisoners in Afghanistan who were being taught new skills.

MUSEUM HISTORY

11

STORIES FROM THE
SECOND WORLD WAR

Tamzine is a humble fishing boat from Kent which got caught up in a daring adventure. She was sent to rescue British soldiers from France on the beaches of Dunkirk in 1940. As the Germans overran France, the British had to try to bring all their soldiers and equipment home, and boats like *Tamzine* helped to save the army.

> 'The scene in the Channel was quite amazing ... there were so many ships there, and it was incredible to us that all this could be going on without the Germans knowing anything about it.'
> Lieutenant-Commander Cromwell Lloyd-Davies, on board HMS *Glasgow* on D-Day, 1944

FIND IT!

One of the pieces of *X-7* was brought up from the fjord in 1976 – you can see it in the Turning Points exhibition on Level 1. Find out more about Godfrey Place and the medal he earned for this mission in the Lord Ashcroft Gallery on Level 5.

THE LAST MISSION OF THE *X-7*

GODFREY PLACE WAS AN OFFICER IN THE ROYAL NAVY. IN SEPTEMBER 1943 HE WAS GIVEN A VERY DANGEROUS MISSION.

HE WAS PUT IN COMMAND OF A MIDGET SUBMARINE CALLED X-7, AND TOLD TO ATTACK A GERMAN BATTLESHIP IN A FJORD IN NORWAY.

THE X-7 MADE IT THROUGH A MINEFIELD AND ANTI-TORPEDO NETS. THE CREW PUT TWO MINES UNDER THE GERMAN SHIP, WHICH CAUSED A LOT OF DAMAGE.

BUT THEN THE X-7 GOT CAUGHT IN THE ANTI-TORPEDO NETS! GODFREY HAD TO BRING HIS SUBMARINE UP TO THE SURFACE AND SURRENDER. BECAUSE HE HAD MANAGED A VERY DIFFICULT MISSION, GODFREY WAS AWARDED THE VICTORIA CROSS FOR HIS BRAVERY.

'What's going to happen to us tonight? Are we going to blow up? Catch fire or get shot down? All those things went through your mind.'

Arnold Easton, who during the Second World War flew in the Lancaster bomber that you can see at the very beginning of this book

British Royal Marine commandos landing in Normandy on D-Day, 1944

This grey metal tube is a small air raid shelter. It was used in the street by people who worked outdoors during bombing raids, like policemen and air raid wardens. A warden could duck inside the shelter and be protected.

On 6 June 1944, called 'D-Day', the Allies invaded north-west Europe to win it back from the Germans. Thousands of British, American and Canadian soldiers went by boat across the Channel from England to France. They were given paper 'vomit bags', in case the rough sea made them sick.

13

STORIES FROM THE
SECOND WORLD WAR

During the war, families were encouraged to build an Anderson shelter in their garden. They had to dig a deep pit, because half the shelter was underground. This protected them from bombs dropped by aircraft.

It was a big step down into the shelter. Once everyone was inside, the entrance was covered over.

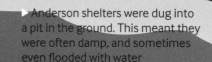

This stirrup pump was used to put out fires at home, caused by the bombs. One person pumped water from the bucket, while another person aimed the hose at the fire.

▶Anderson shelters were dug into a pit in the ground. This meant they were often damp, and sometimes even flooded with water

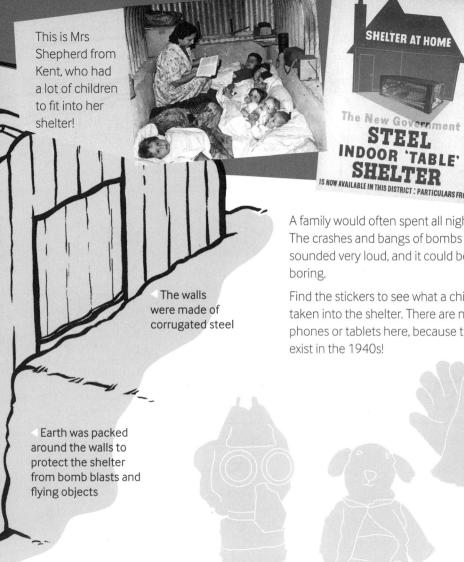

This is Mrs Shepherd from Kent, who had a lot of children to fit into her shelter!

SHELTER AT HOME

The New Government
STEEL INDOOR 'TABLE' SHELTER
IS NOW AVAILABLE IN THIS DISTRICT : PARTICULARS FROM

FIND **IT!**

Not everyone had a garden. Have a look at the Morrison shelter in the Turning Points exhibition on Level 1. This shelter was designed for the house. With its strong frame, it would stay standing even if the house fell down.

STICKER **IT!**

◄ The walls were made of corrugated steel

◄ Earth was packed around the walls to protect the shelter from bomb blasts and flying objects

A family would often spent all night in their shelter. The crashes and bangs of bombs falling nearby sounded very loud, and it could be damp, cold and boring.

Find the stickers to see what a child might have taken into the shelter. There are no mobile phones or tablets here, because they didn't exist in the 1940s!

SECOND WORLD WAR

LEVEL **1**

15

STORIES FROM THE
SECOND WORLD WAR

This painting shows the food that was rationed in 1941. Fruit and vegetables weren't rationed – people could eat as much of these as they could get.

Start a conversation

How much of each of the foods in the painting does your family eat in a week? Would you have to change your diet to fit with rationing?

Coupons Required,
Leonora Green, 1941.

Fun Fact

Nothing could be wasted in wartime. Even old potato peelings could be eaten, though maybe not by people. 'Pig bins' were put on the streets for people to put their waste food into, for feeding pigs.

This is the 'Squander Bug', an ugly cartoon character invented by the government to encourage people not to waste food and other things needed for the war.

The government knew that big cities would probably be bombed. Just before the war started they sent over 800,000 children from the cities to safer places in the countryside. They were called 'evacuees'. They had to wear labels with their names and home addresses. Some had fun in the country, but many were unhappy to be so far away from home.

'When I was evacuated, there were red London double-decker buses ... taking the whole school – teachers and pupils – down to Wokingham. That's about forty miles from London, but it felt like the end of the Earth. I felt very unhappy, it was my first time away from home.'

John Allpress

When she was an evacuee in Kent, a young girl called Dorothy King wrote home to her mum in London. This is the last page of her letter. Can you see what she has drawn?

17

PEACE AND SECURITY

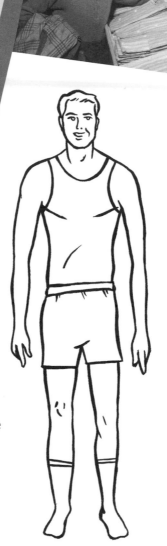

At the end of the Second World War Britain needed lots of houses – and quickly! Many houses had been destroyed by bombs, and now people who had been fighting were coming home. The government ordered 'prefab' houses to be made. These were made in sections in factories, then put together wherever there was space for people to build them.

Newsflash: TV for all!

All television programmes were switched off during the Second World War. TV started up again in 1946. 20 million people watched the coronation of Queen Elizabeth II on TV in 1953.

STICKER IT!

To help men coming back from the war, they were given a demob suit. ('Demobilisation' is a word for leaving the army, air force or navy at the end of a war.) Find the demob clothes in your sticker set, and dress your soldier for his new life!

Joan Oram was given this bag by the Canadian Red Cross at the end of the war, as she made her way home to Britain from Hong Kong where she had been a prisoner. Her son Roger Tolson remembered his mother later using this bag to hold all the family's presents from Santa!

This doll was made by homeless people from Latvia in a camp in Germany after the war. A British man who worked there gave it to his daughter, who thought the doll looked sad. Colour her in, and maybe give her a smile!

COLOUR IT!

education

new knowledge new worlds new pleasures

APPLY TO YOUR ATS EDUCATION OFFICER FOR PARTICULARS OF THE ARMY EDUCATION SCHEME

This poster was for people leaving the British Army after the Second World War. The army offered education schemes to help them get jobs.

When David Harvey was 4 years old he had to leave his London home because of the bombing. When he came back, he was given this scooter. One of the customers in his parents' pub had made it, out of wood from bombed houses in his street, to welcome him home!

PEACE AND SECURITY

LEVEL 2

19

PEACE AND SECURITY

This is a remote-control robot, used to make bombs safe in Northern Ireland. It's called a Morfax Wheelbarrow, because its inventor used parts from a motorised wheelbarrow.
As it has tracks instead of wheels, it can even go up and down stairs!

Five of these bomb casings were made in America for a new atomic bomb known as 'Little Boy'. One of them was dropped on the Japanese city of Hiroshima on 6 August 1945. It was the most powerful bomb there had ever been.

ACTIVITY

Can you get to the bomb to make it safe? Drive down the right path – and hurry!

FIND
IT!

Can you see this piece of the Berlin Wall outside the museum?

The wall divided the German city of Berlin in two from 1961 to 1989. Lots of people celebrated when the wall came down and they were free to once again move around the whole city.

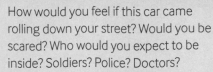

How would you feel if this car came rolling down your street? Would you be scared? Who would you expect to be inside? Soldiers? Police? Doctors?

The United Nations used this vehicle in the 1980s to patrol the border that separated the Turkish and Greek people on the island of Cyprus.

'I could give you the government line to it. But we are soldiers. We chose to do the job and really it's the age-old saying: "You don't go somewhere to fight for your Queen and country, it's more you're out there to cover your mate's back"'.
Billy Moore, soldier in Afghanistan

This poster is silly, but also serious. It was designed in 2004 as a protest against war in Iraq. The man with a teacup on his head like a helmet is Tony Blair, who was the British Prime Minister at the time. How does the poster make him look?

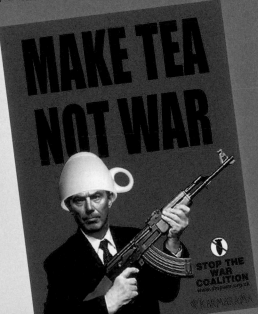

MAKE TEA NOT WAR

STOP THE WAR COALITION
www.stopwar.org.uk

21

SECRET WAR

Special Operations Executive (SOE) was a British secret unit set up to fight the Germans in Europe and to help people resist the Nazis. They invented all sorts of sneaky tricks to play on the Germans. An agent called Ben Cowburn even put itching powder inside German uniforms!

Suitcase radios like this were used in the Second World War by SOE agents in occupied France, to help them stay in touch with Britain. If an agent was caught with a radio, they could be shot – so radio operators had the most dangerous job in SOE!

FIND IT!

In the Lord Ashcroft Gallery on Level 5, look out for Odette Sansom – a French woman who worked with SOE in France. You can see her jacket and guns, and dolls that she made in prison.

NOOR AGAINST THE GERMANS

NOOR INAYAT KHAN GREW UP IN PARIS. HER FATHER WAS INDIAN AND HER MOTHER WAS AMERICAN. WHEN THE GERMANS INVADED FRANCE, NOOR'S FAMILY CAME TO ENGLAND.

SHE JOINED SOE AND WAS SENT TO FRANCE AS A RADIO OPERATOR. HER JOB WAS VERY DANGEROUS. IF THE NAZIS FOUND HER RADIO, SHE WOULD BE SHOT.

ONE DAY NOOR WAS ON A TRAIN WHEN TWO GERMAN OFFICERS ASKED WHAT WAS IN HER CASE...

CINEMA EQUIPMENT

LUCKILY THE GERMANS BELIEVED HER.

IN 1944 NOOR WAS KILLED BY THE NAZIS. HER LAST WORD WAS 'LIBERTÉ' - FRENCH FOR 'FREEDOM'. TO HONOUR HER BRAVERY SHE WAS AWARDED THE GEORGE CROSS.

Lots of spy kit isn't what it seems. This pen is actually a gadget for finding 'bugs', which are used to listen in on people's conversations.

One match in this box has a special top which can be used for secret writing. It was found on a German spy in Britain in the First World War.

'... [the Auxiliary Units] would have been coming out at night, blowing up an odd bridge, knocking off a factory, wherever they could injure the enemy.'
William Pilkington, self-defence instructor for the Auxiliary Units

During the Second World War a top-secret British force was trained to use explosives and to kill without normal weapons. Very few people knew about them. Known as the Auxiliary Units, they would have caused a lot of trouble for the Germans if Britain had been invaded and occupied.

Hidden in this section of a gate post from Devon, there is a secret letterbox. It was designed for the Auxiliary Units to pass secret messages to each other.

SECRET WAR

23

ART

IWM has almost 20,000 paintings, drawings, sculptures and other artworks in its collection. The art on display in the museum changes all the time. What will you see on your visit?

The painting below shows British Air Force fighter pilots defending Britain from an attack by German planes. When the Germans fight the British over the sea, the battle makes great swooping shapes.

In 1940 the Germans tried to destroy the British Air Force, but the British fought back in the skies over southern England – and won. This was known as the Battle of Britain.

Women's Canteen at Phoenix Works, Bradford, Flora Lion, 1918

In the First World War over a million women worked in factories making ammunition for British guns.

Do you think the women in the painting look tired? Is it early in the day? Are they happy to be working?

Battle of Britain, Paul Nash, 1941

Fun Fact

Art is important, even when there's a war on. The British government started appointing official War Artists in the First World War, to show people at home what the war was like. Since those days War Artists have travelled all over the world!

War Artist Linda Kitson sketched soldiers during the Falklands War in the 1980s. Can you see a pair of boots? Who do you think has just taken them off? Linda's packing for the war included a folding stool and damp-proof oil pencils so she could draw in the rain.

2nd Battalion Scots Guards in the Sheep Sheds at Fitzroy, 17 June 1982,
Linda Kitson, 1982

FIND IT!

You can see some things Linda Kitson took with her to the Falklands in the Peace and Security exhibition on Level 2. Find her warm jacket, her watertight container and more of her drawings.

DRAW IT!

Use this space to create your own war art. You could copy one of the artworks on display, or draw your favourite object from your visit to the museum.

Don't forget to add your name!

ART

EXTRAORDINARY HEROES
THE LORD ASHCROFT GALLERY

The White Rabbit was the codename for a Second World War secret agent called Forest Yeo-Thomas. He was awarded the George Cross for his courage.

▶ He was captured by the Nazis and tortured, but refused to tell them anything.

▶ Next he was kept away from other prisoners in solitary confinement for four months — so he sang cheery songs about Britain to annoy his guards. And tried to escape, twice.

▶ When he was sent to a concentration camp to be killed, he swapped his identity with a sick prisoner who was dying. He kept on causing trouble for the Germans.

▶ He was sent to two more camps — and escaped from both of them!

FIND IT!

See the White Rabbit's fake identity card ✓

FRED POTTS
AND THE LIFE-SAVING SHOVEL

FRED POTTS WAS A BRITISH SOLDIER IN THE FIRST WORLD WAR. IN 1915 HE WAS SENT TO GALLIPOLI IN TURKEY TO FIGHT AGAINST THE TURKISH ARMY.

FRED AND HIS REGIMENT ATTACKED THE TURKS AT SCIMITAR HILL. THEY HAD TO CHARGE UPHILL IN THE HEAT. FRED WAS SHOT IN THE LEG, AND FELL TO THE GROUND.

HE HID IN THE BUSHES WITH ANOTHER WOUNDED MAN, ARTHUR ANDREWS. THEY HID FOR A DAY AND A HALF WITH NO FOOD OR WATER, CRAWLING DOWN THE HILL AT NIGHT.

BY THE SECOND NIGHT ARTHUR WAS TOO HURT TO MOVE. FRED FOUND A SHOVEL AND TIED ARTHUR TO IT - THEN STOOD UP, WITH BULLETS FLYING AROUND HIM, AND DRAGGED HIS FRIEND TO SAFETY. THEY BOTH SURVIVED. FRED WAS GIVEN THE VICTORIA CROSS FOR HIS BRAVERY.

Johnson Beharry was driving armoured vehicles in Iraq in 2004 when he was ambushed by the enemy – twice. Each time he rescued the other men in his unit. The first time he was shot in the head. On his helmet you can see the hole the bullet made, and the names of the friends whose lives he saved. The second time a rocket hit Johnson's head and he nearly died.

The helmet which saved Johnson's life on 1 May 2004

Could you give your life for someone else's? John Quinton did. In 1951 his RAF plane crashed in mid-air. John grabbed the only parachute and strapped it to 16-year-old Derek Coates. Derek survived to tell the story. John Quinton was awarded the George Cross, which was given to his widow.

EXTRAORDINRY HEROES

LEVEL 5

STICKER IT!

This gallery was opened in 2010 to display Lord Ashcroft's collection of Victoria Cross and George Cross medals. Find the Victoria Cross and George Cross stickers and stick them on the shapes below.

▶ The Victoria Cross is given for bravery in battle

Do you know anyone who you think deserves a medal for bravery?

◀ The George Cross is given for bravery in either peacetime or wartime situations

This is the girl who fought a mountain lion in Canada and won! In 1916, when Doreen Ashburnham was 11 years old, she and her cousin were attacked by a mountain lion, known as a cougar. She jumped on the cougar's back and stuck her arm in its mouth to protect her cousin. It finally gave up and both children went home, injured but with a fantastic story to tell! The children were given the Albert Medal (an earlier version of the George Cross), which Doreen is wearing in the photo.

27

THE CONSERVATION LAB

Lots goes on behind the scenes at IWM. The conservation team make sure that objects in the museum can tell their stories for many years to come.

▶ **Bug poster**
To identify bugs caught around the museum

BUG INDENTIFICATION

▶ **Book press**
This makes flat things flatter, like old letters that have got damp and wrinkled

! DANGER

There are dangers lurking in the IWM stores. Old medical kits sometimes contain dangerous drugs; paint used on radio dials can be radioactive; cancer-causing asbestos can be found hiding in First World War gas masks. The conservation team make everything safe.

▶ **Shipping crate**
To hold objects for touring exhibitions around the world. Very careful packing skills are needed

FRAGILE

Woolly bears are a big threat to the museum's collections. No, really! That's the nickname for the young carpet beetle. They munch their way through fabric and love anywhere dusty or where bits of hair gather. So you have to clean under your bed if you want to avoid the terrible Woolly Bear!

Fun Fact

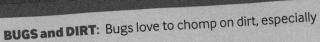
Know your Enemies!

BUGS and DIRT: Bugs love to chomp on dirt, especially in dark corners

FIGHT IT: Keep objects in airtight showcases; keep things clean; if bugs attack an object, freeze it

HEAT, COLD, DAMP and DRY: These damage all sorts of materials

FIGHT THEM: Keep the heating in the museum at an even level; seal objects in showcases; use silica gel to soak up moisture from the air

LIGHT: Ultra-violet light weakens many materials

FIGHT IT: Use special lightbulbs to filter out harmful rays of light. Keep very fragile objects out of the light

ACID: When paper gets old, acid starts to form which makes it weaker

FIGHT IT: Wash your paper – very carefully!

▼ Blender and microwave
The Conservation team use these to make a kind of glue called wheat starch paste, used to repair paper

▲ Solvent pots
These are special safe pots for keeping solvents, which are chemicals used for cleaning things like metal and for making glues

▲ Sticky trap
For catching insects. This is how the conservators find out if bugs are living in the IWM buildings!

◄ Using a microscope
The conservation team use this for looking closely at bugs, or for looking to see what objects are made of and what condition they are in

THE CONSERVATION LAB

LEVEL

2

29

FOR GROWN-UPS TALKING TO CHILDREN ABOUT WAR

▶ Children find out about war in the news as well as from friends and family — sometimes sooner than their parents would like. You may find that your visit to IWM London helps your family to start talking about difficult subjects like war.

▶ There are several discussion prompts in this guidebook, marked 'Start a Conversation'. You may not feel able to talk about these at length in the museum. If your child is interested, try finding a quiet, safe space to talk once you're at home.

▶ Instead of leading the conversation yourself, try asking open questions to find out what your child thinks and if they have any concerns. Try to be reassuring, but open.

▶ Explore together to find out more. On the IWM website click on the Research button to look up objects you'd like to know more about. There are also useful summaries of key topics on our 'Collections in Context' pages. You can also use the BBC History website for reference.

* The Holocaust exhibition is not featured in this guidebook, as it is not recommended for under-14s. If you would like to introduce your younger child to the subject of the Holocaust, we run special learning sessions in small groups. Please ask for details at the reception desk, phone the museum on +44 (0)20 7416 5000, or visit the website at iwm.org.uk

OTHER IWM BRANCHES

IWM NORTH

IWM's home in Manchester is housed in a dramatic building which represents how the world is shattered by war. It has permanent and temporary exhibitions which tell stories from conflicts since the First World War.

HMS *BELFAST*

IWM owns a Second World War warship on the Thames in London. Explore the nine decks to find out about life at sea and at war in the Second World War and afterwards.

DUXFORD

If IWM London's Spitfire and Lancaster cockpit left you wanting more, IWM Duxford is perfect. In an airbase near Cambridge, begun in the First World War, you'll find fascinating stories about the history of flying, as well as many objects that are too big to be on show in IWM's other museums.

CHURCHILL WAR ROOMS

This is the underground bunker where Churchill's government worked during the Blitz. Find out how the Cabinet operated here in secret from 1940 to 1945, and visit the museum dedicated to Prime Minister Winston Churchill.

All images © IWM unless otherwise stated

Published by IWM, Lambeth Road, London SE1 6HZ
5th edition, 2019
© The Trustees of the Imperial War Museum, 2019

All rights reserved. No part of this publication may be reproduced, stored in a retrieval system or transmitted in any form or by any means electronic, mechanical, photocopying, recording or otherwise without the prior permission of the copyright holder and publisher.

ISBN: 978-1-904897-56-9
Printed by Belmont Press, UK

The publishers will be glad to make good in future editions any error or omissions brought to their attention.

Our thanks to Jo Foster (author), HL Studios (design), Frances Castle (map and comic strip illustrations), Darren Baxter (drawings on pp 14-15, 18, 28-29) and all IWM staff involved in this book.

Inside front cover: UNI 12917 1 A, EQU 4509 A, EPH 9032 B, 2010 20 6, 2010 285 1 B; pp 2–3: IWM SITE LAM 3474, IWM SITE LAM 3469, IWM SITE LAM 3473; pp 4–5: MUN 3853 A, IWM SITE LAM 3473, ORD 102 B, 2010 30 8 A, SPACEVAC 8, DE 1032 A; pp 6–7: IWM PST 2734, EPH 2937 A, Documents.13978 J 1, IWM ART 2243, COM 1068, FEQ 854, Q 50669; pp 8–9: EPH 3797, Docments.17742, MOD 2272; pp 10–11: Documents. 8012, MH 127, IWM ART 303, UNI 11312 A, WS 1028 B, WS 1029 E, DC 4139; pp 12–13: MAR 556 5, A 21799, FEQ 485, UNI 12917 1 A, 2010 20 6, B 5245, EPH 4435 13; pp 14–15: ZZZ 9182 C, FEQ 418, D 778, IWM PST 13855, EPH 2216, EPH 2540, UNI 12834, EQU 3643 1 B, Access 13 1330 1; pp 16–17: IWM ART 16344, EPH 4611, D 2593, KingDE 6803 4; pp 18–19: HU 66232, TR 1580, TV SET 3, EPH 10943, IWM PST 2943, EPH 9958 B, EPH 10264 A; pp 20–21: MUN 3845 A, 4109 100 A, UNI 12387, UNI 13161, bomb image © Shutterstock, EPH 467, 4104 48 3 A, IWM PST 8815 © Karmarama; pp 22–23: COM 229, HU 74868, COM 1506, EPH 178, EPH 10074; pp 24–25: IWM ART 4434, IWM ART LD 1550, IWM ART 15530 52; 26–27: HU 98898, Documents.17363 T, YeoThomas FFE 12653 12, UNI 13826 F, HU 3161, OMD 2406 1. OMD 3131, Johnson Beharry portrait © Getty Images; pp 28–29: IWM SITE LAM 2417, IWM SITE LAM 4117, LAB 001, LAB 009, LAB 010, LAB 011; pp 30–31: IWM SITE LAM 2110, IWM SITE IWMN 1275, IWM 2014 071 222 vs2, IWM SITE BELF 748, IWM SITE CWR 448.

 **QUIZ** Answer this quiz to see how much you've found out from your visit to IWM London. Can you remember any of the answers without looking them up?

1 How many objects does IWM have in its collections? (Answer on p.2)

....

2 What is the name of the stuffed pig in the First World War gallery? (Answer on inside cover)

....

3 What do the Conservation team use to clean the hanging aeroplanes? (Answer on p.5)

....

4 Which 9-year-old boy wrote to Lord Kitchener to volunteer for the Front? (Answer on p.6)

....

5 Who sent presents to everyone fighting for Britain in 1914? (Answer on p.8)

....

6 Which country did an IWM collecting team visit in 2012–14? (Answer on p.11)

....

7 What kind of air raid shelter did the Allpress family have in their garden? (Answer on p.14)

....

8 What do you call a child who was sent to the countryside for safety in the Second World War? (Answer on p.17)

....

9 Which piece of garden equipment gave its name to a bomb disposal robot? (Answer on p.20)

....

10 What did SOE agent Ben Cowburn put in German uniforms to annoy them? (Answer on p.22)

....

11 What job did Linda Kitson do in the Falklands War in 1982? (Answer on p.25)

....

12 What did Fred Potts use to save his friend's life in the First World War? (Answer on p.26)

....

Page 8

Page 15

Page 18

Page 27